# Englisl . Together

## Pupils' Book 2

**Diana Webster and Anne Worrall**

Longman

# *Language syllabus*

| Unit | Main teaching points | Main revision |
|---|---|---|
| **1** | | was/were<br>*Questions.*<br>*Pronouns:* I/you/he/she/they<br>*Present simple.*<br>*Present continuous.*<br>*Colours.*<br>*Numbers* |
| **2** | that | this<br>*Family.*<br>*Possessive* 's.<br>have/has got<br>*Present simple.*<br>*Days of the week.*<br>*Descriptions of people.*<br>There is/are/was/were . . .<br>in/on/under<br>*Furniture.*<br>can . . . (*ability*) |
| **3** | *Past simple: regular verbs.*<br>went<br>then<br>*Rooms in a house.* | *Present continuous.*<br>*Present simple.*<br>How many?<br>was/were<br>*Prepositions.* |
| **4** | What/Where did . . . ?<br>want to<br>these | *Present simple.*<br>*Past simple.*<br>*Family.*<br>Do/Does . . . ? |
| **5** | those<br>Did you/he/she/they . . .?<br>didn't<br>but | that<br>*Past simple.*<br>What did . . . ?<br>afraid of . . .<br>*Food.*<br>*Telling the time.* |
| **6**<br>REVISION | *Months.* | *Past simple.*<br>*Present simple.*<br>*Rooms in a house.*<br>*Possessive* 's.<br>What . . . like?<br>this/these, that/those<br>*Days of the week.*<br>can |
| **7** | *Asking and talking about height.*<br>*The alphabet and spelling.*<br>*Imperatives.*<br>*Large numbers:* Hundreds and thousands. | *Numbers.*<br>*Talking about age.*<br>want to . . .<br>*Prepositions.*<br>*Past simple.* |

| Unit | Main teaching points | Main revision |
|---|---|---|
| **8** | *Future tense with 'going to'.*<br>Which?<br>When?<br>*Jobs.* | *Present continuous.*<br>like/don't like . . .<br>want to . . .<br>*Telling the time.*<br>*Numbers.*<br>*Spelling.* |
| **9** | Let's . . . !<br>*Pronouns:* it/him/her/them<br>Why?/Because . . .<br>this/that/these/those (*Adjectival*) | *Past simple.*<br>*Future tense with 'going to'.*<br>this/these |
| **10**<br>REVISION | | *The alphabet.*<br>*Future tense with 'going to'.*<br>*Pronouns.*<br>*Past simple.*<br>*Telling the time.*<br>*Prepositions.*<br>there is/are/was/were |
| **11** | our/their<br>Whose?<br>Can . . . (*permission*)<br>a (piece) of . . .<br>always/sometimes | *Past simple.*<br>*Possessive* 's.<br>*Food.*<br>*Descriptions of people.*<br>Why/Because . . .<br>Present continuous. |
| **12** | *Telling the time:*<br>half/quarter past/to<br>*Nationalities.*<br>*Prepositions:* next to/<br>behind/in front of | Which?<br>When?<br>*Present simple.*<br>*Past simple.*<br>*Countries.*<br>want to . . . |
| **13** | some/any<br>*Animals.* | *Past simple.*<br>Have you/has she got . . . ?<br>Are there . . . ?<br>*Present simple.*<br>*Questions.*<br>Why/Because . . .<br>*Imperatives.* |
| **14** | somebody/anybody<br>By car/bus/train/plane<br>*Talking about the weather.* | *Future tense with 'going to'*<br>*Weather.*<br>*Countries.*<br>*Imperatives.* |
| **15**<br>REVISION | | *Descriptions of people.*<br>*Telling the time.*<br>*Past simple.*<br>*Prepositions.*<br>*The Alphabet and spelling.* |

# Unit 1

## 1 Happy holidays

| | |
|---|---|
| Listen and look | It's winter. Beth, Joe, Al and Emma are going to Scotland. |
| Read | They are in a train. |
| Act | They are looking at photos. |

Emma: Where were you in the summer holidays, Al?
Al: I was in the mountains. Where were you?

Emma: My sister and I were by the sea.

Joe: My friends Sara and Tom and I were in the country.

Emma: Were you in the country, too, Beth?
Beth: No, I was at home. It was fun!

## 2 Where were they?

Listen

Ask and answer

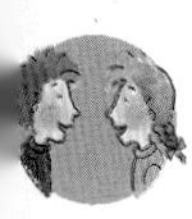

**A:** Where was Al?
**B:** He was in the mountains.

**B:** Where were Emma and her sister?
**A:** They were by the sea.

## 3 Joe's holiday photos

Listen and look

Read

## 4 Questions

Read

Ask and answer

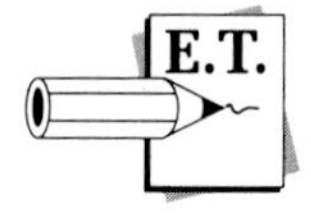


Read about Joe's holiday pictures.
Ask your partner questions.

Picture **1** What is Sara doing? She . . .
Picture **2** What are Tom and Sara doing? They . . .
Picture **3** What has Sara got in her hand?
Picture **4** What are Tom and Sara making?
Picture **5** Where are they?

Now write the answers in your ET book.

## 5 What are you doing?

Listen

Play

| | | | |
|---|---|---|---|
| swim | play football | climb | read |
| run | make hamburgers | write | jump |

## 6 I love holidays

Listen

Sing

Climbing in the mountains,
Swimming in the sea,
Happy, happy holidays,
For you and me.
I love, you love,
He loves, she loves,
We all love holidays.
Happy, happy holidays,
We all love, we all love
holiday time!

Playing on the beaches,
Sitting in the sun,
Happy, happy holidays,
Lots of fun.
I love . . .

# Unit 2

## 1 Cliff Castle

Listen and look

Read

Act

The children are in Scotland.
Al's uncle lives there.

Al: Look! That's Cliff Castle!
Beth: Does your uncle live in a castle?
Al: Yes.
Beth: Great!

Al: This is my uncle Colin.
Colin: Hello. Come in, everyone.

| | |
|---|---|
| Al: | That's my cousin Tammy. |
| Beth: | How old is she? |
| Al: | She's three, nearly four. |
| | And that's her cat. |
| Joe: | What's her name? |
| Al: | Cleo. |
| Joe: | Hello, Cleo. |
| Emma: | What's that? |
| Colin: | That's the ghost. |
| Joe: | Is there a ghost in the castle? |
| Colin: | Wait and see! |

## 2 Who's that?

Listen

Ask and answer

**1** grandpa

**2** uncle

**3** aunt

**4** cousin

| | |
|---|---|
| Beth: | Who's that? |
| Joe: | That's Al's grandpa. |

## 3 Al's cousins

Listen

Say

Ask
and answer

1

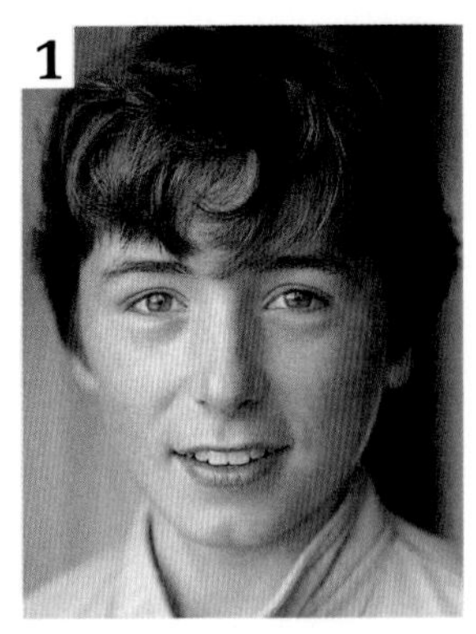

This is Sam.
He's fourteen.
He lives in
Dublin.
That's in
Ireland.

2

Fiona is ten.
She lives in
Glasgow.
That's in Scotland.

3

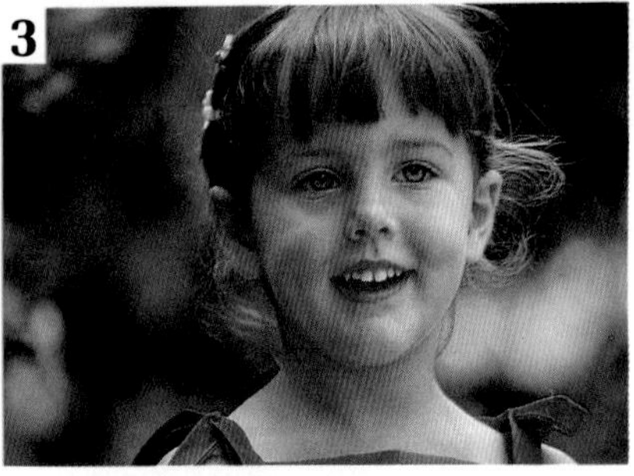

This is Jenny.
She's five.
She lives in Cardiff.
That's in Wales.

4

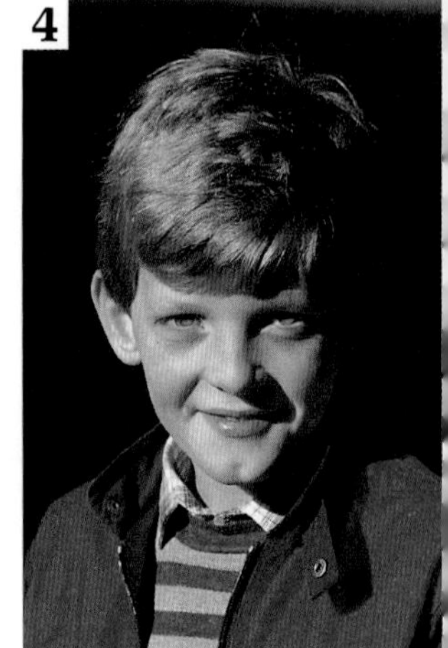

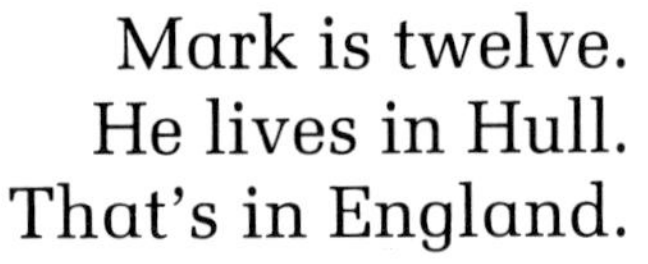

Mark is twelve.
He lives in Hull.
That's in England.

Beth: What's his name?
Al: Sam.
Beth: How old is he?
Al: He's fourteen.
Beth: Where does he live?
Al: In Dublin.
Beth: Where's that?
Al: In Ireland.

## 4 How many bats?

Look

Read

Say

This is a room in Cliff Castle.
How many bats are there?
How many spiders are there?
Where are they?

There is a spider on the green chair.
There are two bats under the table and . . .

Listen

Ask and answer

Partner **A**, ask **B** three questions about the picture.
**B**, close your book. Can you remember?

**A:** Was there a spider under the green chair? **B:** Yes.
**A:** Were there four bats under the table? **B:** No.

# Factfile
## Scotland

There are four countries in Britain. They are England, Wales, Scotland and Northern Ireland.

This is Scotland.

Scotland is a very beautiful country. There are high mountains and big lakes. In winter you can ski in the mountains. There are lots of castles in Scotland.

People in Scotland sometimes wear kilts. They play bagpipes and they dance.

Write about your country in your ET book.

In North Scotland there is a deep, dark lake – Loch Ness. People say there is a big monster in the lake – the Loch Ness Monster.

What is it? Is it a dinosaur? Is it a dragon? Is it a huge snake? Is it a monster? Or is it only a tree? Nobody knows.

Here is a photo. People think it is the Loch Ness Monster. What do you think? Can you see a head? Can you see a long neck? Can you see a body?

# Are the dinosaurs all dead?

**One night in 1934, Arthur Grant, a student, was on his motorbike near Loch Ness. Suddenly the monster was there on the road in front of Arthur's bike. He says, 'It was about six metres long. Its neck was very long and its legs were like a huge seal's legs. I think it was a plesiosaur.'**

A plesiosaur is a dinosaur. Scientists say it is extinct. They say the last plesiosaur was on the earth seventy million years ago. What do you think?

Draw the monster in your ET book. Write about it. How many legs has it got? Are they long or short? Has it got a tail? Has it got big teeth? What colour is it?

# Unit 3

## 1 The secret room

Listen and look

Read

Act

Yesterday was rainy. Beth and Joe watched TV in the living room.

Then Joe wanted a book. He looked on the bookshelf.

Joe pressed the button.

The door opened.

They went in.
It was a secret room.

Beth looked at the giant computer.

Beth pressed a key.

## 2 What happened?

Listen

Ask
and answer

**A:** What happened in picture 2?
**B:** Joe pressed a button.

**B:** What happened in picture 3?
**A:** The door opened.

Now ask and answer about pictures **4**, **5** and **6**.

# 3 Rooms in Cliff Castle

Listen and look

Read

Practise

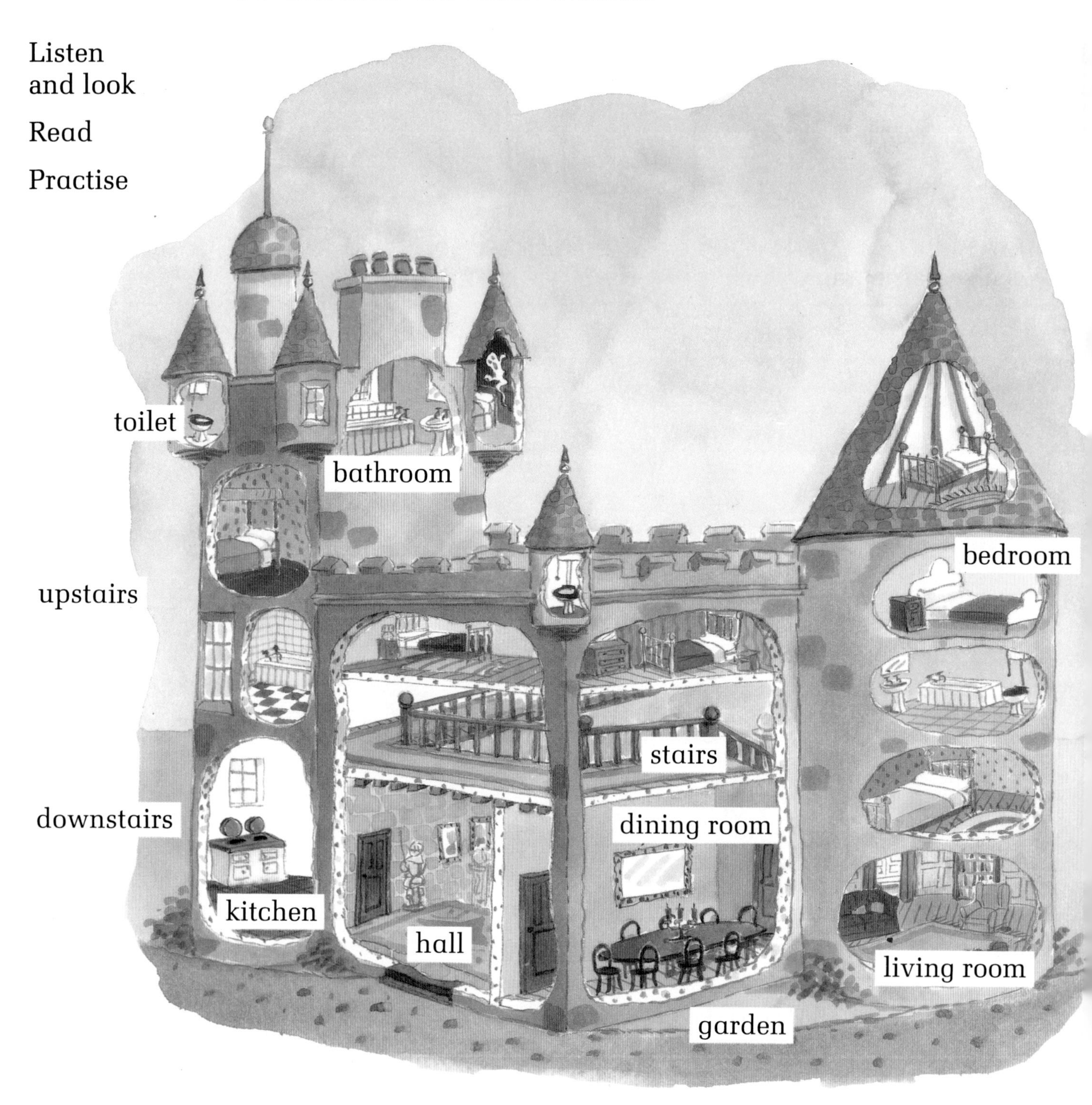


How many rooms can you see?
How many bedrooms can you see?
How many toilets?

## 4 Where do you live?

Listen

Say

Sally: Do you live in the town or in the country?
Tim: I live in the town.
Sally: Do you live in a house or a flat?
Tim: In a flat.
Sally: What's it like?
Tim: It's small. There are two bedrooms, a living room, a kitchen, a bathroom and a toilet.

Ask and answer

Ask and answer with a friend.

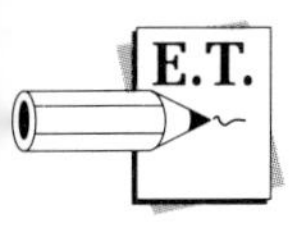


In your ET book, draw your house or flat.
Write the rooms on your picture.

## 5 Play a game

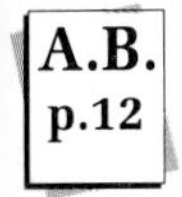


Look at your Action Book.
Draw the animals in the rooms in your picture.
Partner **A**, look at **B**'s picture
Then don't look.

Listen

Ask and answer

# Unit 4

## 1 The computer

Listen and look

Read

Act

Beth and Joe were in the secret room.

Joe: Who's that? What did you do, Beth?
Beth: I pressed these keys. Just a minute . . .

Beth typed her name.

3

Today's games:
Space
Dragons
Treasure hunt

4

Computer: These are today's games.
What game do you want to play?
Beth: 'Space', please.
Computer: Where do you want to go?
Beth: I want to go to a new planet.
Computer: Pick up the black box.
Then stand in the circle.
Press the red button on the box.

5

Joe: What happened? Where are we?
Beth: We're in a spaceship . . . and Tammy and Cleo are here too!

## 2 What do they want to do?

Look and say

**1** They want to fish.

**2** She wants . . .

**3** He . . .

**4**

## 3 What's this? What are these?

Listen

Practise

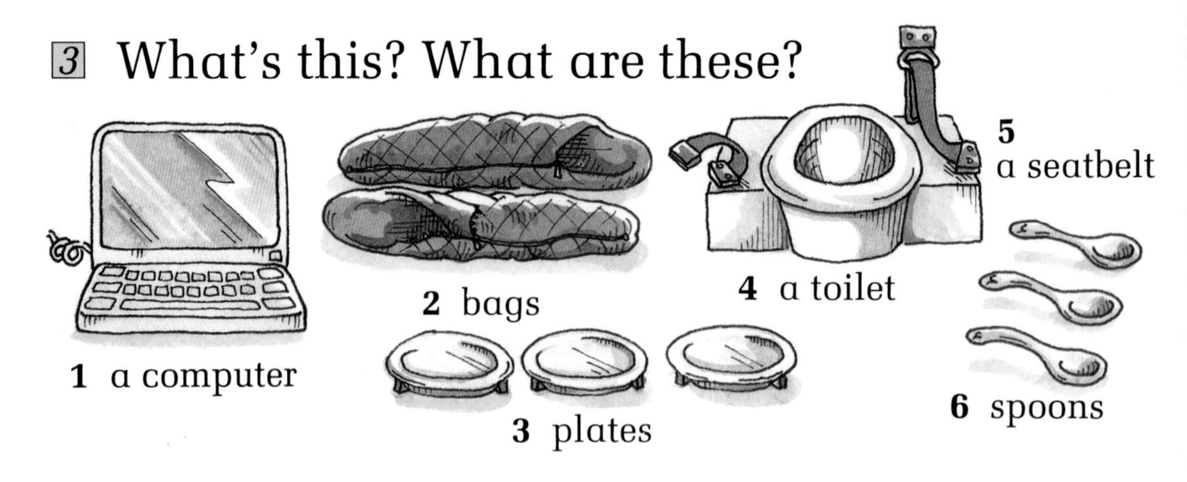


**A:** What's this?
**B:** It's a computer.

**A:** What are these?
**B:** They're bags.

## 4 What did they do?

Listen and look

Read

Look at the pictures.

**1** Monday

Tammy and Cleo watched TV.

**2** Tuesday

Emma listened to music.

**3** Wednesday

Beth and Joe played a computer game.

**4** Thursday

Uncle Colin washed his car.

**5** Friday

Al cleaned his room.

**6** Saturday

The children went to the shops.

Listen

Ask and answer

Partner **A**, close your book and answer **B**'s questions.

**B:** What did Beth and Joe do on Wednesday?
**A:** They played a computer game.

## 5 On the way to school

Listen

Sing

I went to school one morning and
  I walked like this,
I walked like this,
I walked like this.
I went to school one morning
  and I walked like this,
On the way to school.

I saw a rabbit
  and it jumped like this,
It jumped like this . . .

I saw a monkey
  and it climbed like this . . .

I saw my teacher
  and I RAN like this . . .

## 6 Zog the frog

Listen

Say

Zog the frog
  wears long, blue socks.
And eats hot dogs
  from an orange box.

# Factfile
## Astronauts and space

*Space quiz*

Can you answer these questions?

1 What was the first animal in space?
2 Who was the first woman in space?
3 Do astronauts sleep in beds?
4 Can you wash with water in space?
5 How do astronauts keep fit?

Now read and find out.

The first man in space was Yuri Gagarin. He was Russian.

These were the first men on the moon. They were American.

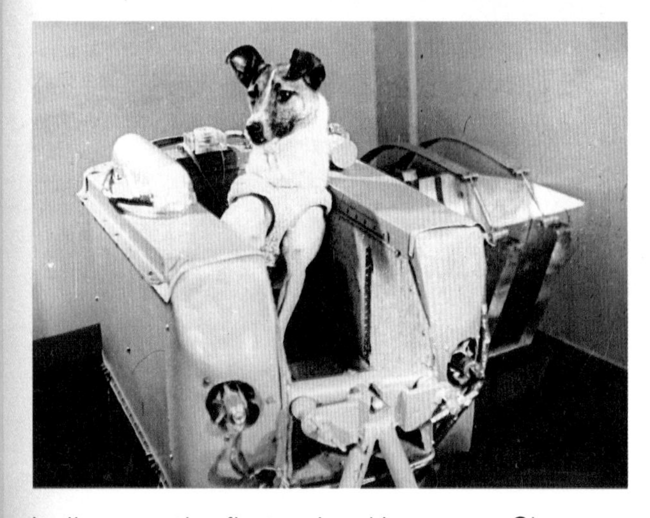

Laika was the first animal in space. She was a Russian dog.

The first woman in space was Valentina Tereshkova.

Astronauts come back to the Earth with thin legs and fat faces!

Astronauts grow five centimetres in space.

*Sleeping in space*

This is a sleep station. Four astronauts can sleep here. One sleeps upside down and one sleeps standing up.

*Keeping clean*

This is a washbasin. There are two holes for hands. Inside there is soap and water.

A child in America suggested a spider in space. Arabella, the space spider, soon made perfect webs.

*Eating in space*

This is the 'kitchen'. There are over a hundred different foods. There is a food pack for every meal. The astronauts eat on trays. Magnets hold the trays down on a table. Magnets hold knives, forks and spoons, too.

*Keeping fit*

Astronauts keep fit in space with a walking-machine.

Draw a spaceship in your ET book. What's in your spaceship? Write about it.

# Unit 5

## 1 The new planet

Listen and look

Read

Act

The children were in a spaceship. They looked out and saw the world – the planet Earth.

Joe: I can see Africa . . . and India . . . and Australia . . .
Beth: . . . and that's the sea . . . and those are mountains . . .
Joe: Did you see that? It was a satellite.
Beth: I didn't see it.
Tammy: I saw it! I saw it!

Tammy jumped up and down.
She liked the spaceship.
Cleo didn't like it.

Suddenly they saw a planet. It was big
nd yellow and it had a rainbow round
t. It was beautiful.

The spaceship landed. They were on a
ew planet!

| | |
|---|---|
| oe: | What are those? |
| Beth: | They're flowers – giant flowers. |
| Tammy: | Are those trees? |
| Beth: | No, they're giant mushrooms. |
| oe: | Wow! |
| Beth: | Where's Cleo? She isn't here. |

## 2 What's that? What are those?

isten

ractise

**1** the Earth

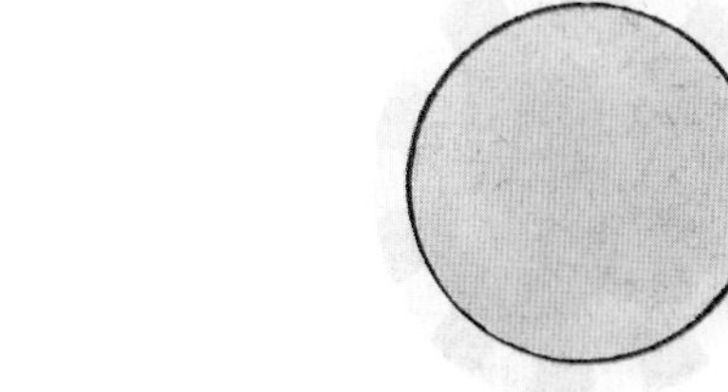

**2** the Sun

**3** the Moon

**4** mountains

**5** clouds

**6** stars

| | |
|---|---|
| Beth: | What's that? |
| Joe: | It's the Earth. |

| | |
|---|---|
| Beth: | What are those? |
| Joe: | They're mountains. |

## 3 Did you see a plane?

Listen

Practise

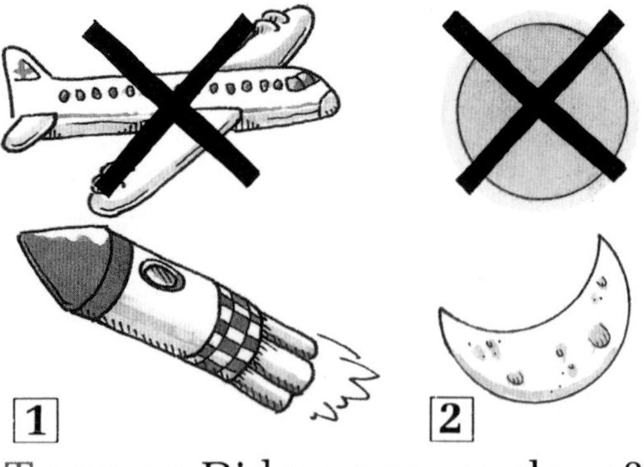

1 2 3 4

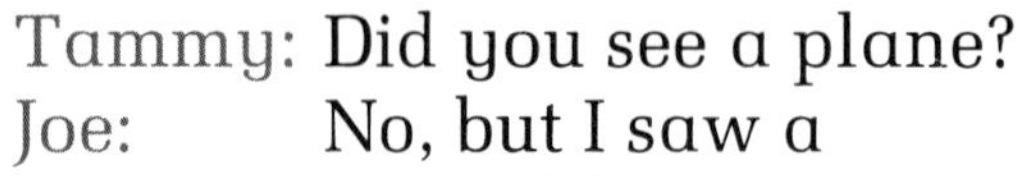

Tammy: Did you see a plane?
Joe: No, but I saw a spaceship.

Tammy: Did you see satellites?

## 4 What didn't they have in the old days?

Listen

Look and say

What's wrong?

**A:** What didn't they have in the old days?
**B:** They didn't have spaceships.

**A:** What did they have?
**B:** They had horses.

## 5 Come with me to the stars!

Listen
Sing

Up in the sky the planets are turning,
The Moon and Venus and Mars.
Up in the sky the stars are shining,
Come with me to the stars!
High, high
Up in the sky,
Far, far
To the furthest star,
Come with me to the stars,
To the stars!
Come with me to the stars!

Up in the sky my spaceship is flying,
The Earth is a tiny ball.
Up in the sky new worlds are waiting,
Listen and hear the stars call!
High, high
Up in the sky . . .

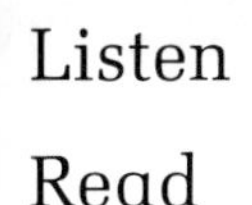

## 6 What happened on the planet?

Listen
Read

The children looked for Cleo. Where was she?

Suddenly there was an awful noise – and then they saw Cleo! She was on a mushroom and there were three giant mice round it. She was afraid.

Cleo jumped down and ran to the children. But a mouse saw the children, too.

'The mice are coming!' said Joe. 'Quick! Press the green button!'

Beth pressed the button – and they were back in the castle.

'That was lucky!' said Tammy.

# Unit 6

## 1 More secrets!

Listen and look

Read

Act

The children ran to Al's uncle.

Al: Are there more secrets in the castle?
Colin: Look and see.

Emma looked in the bathroom. She found a machine in the bath.

Emma: What does it do?
Colin: It washes your back.

Beth looked in the living room.

Beth: What does this do?
Colin: It cleans the room.

Joe looked in the bedroom.

Joe: What does this do?
Colin: It makes the beds.

Al looked in the garden.

Al: What does this do?
Colin: It takes the dog for a walk.

Listen

Ask and answer

clean – cleaned
take – took
make – made

## 2 What did it do?

**A:** Where did Emma find a machine?
**B:** In the bathroom.

**A:** What did it do?
**B:** It washed your back.

## 3 Uncle Colin's camera

Look

Uncle Colin has got a new camera.
These are Tammy's pictures.

**Cleo** **Uncle Colin's kangaroo** **Uncle Colin's parrot**

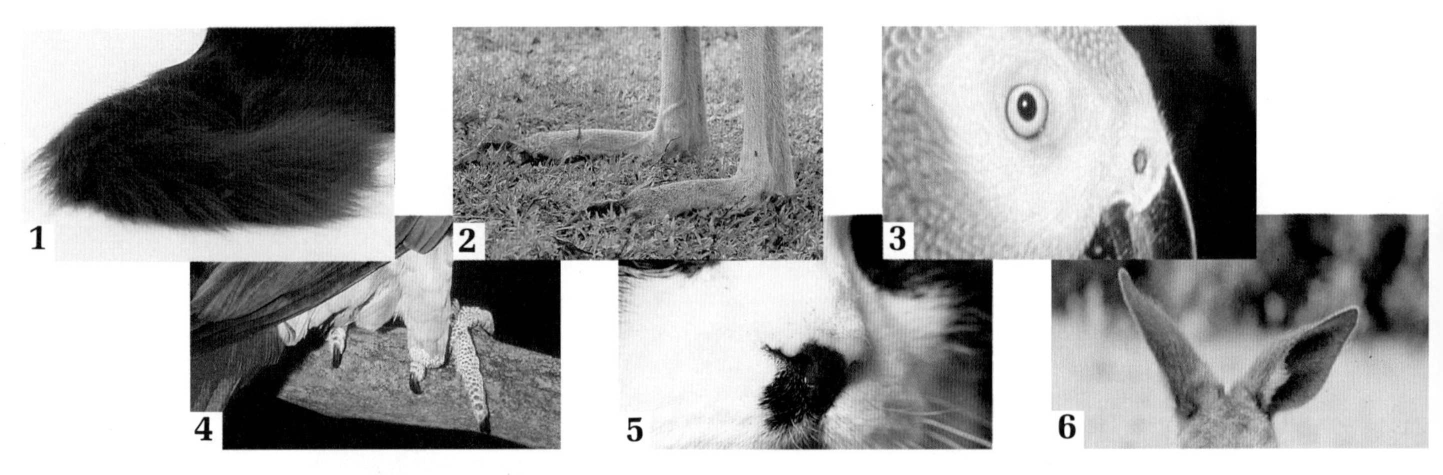


Listen

Ask and answer

**A:** What's this?
**B:** It's Cleo's tail.

**B:** What are these?
**A:** They're the kangaroo's legs.

## 4 The months

Listen

Sing

Take January, February, March,
With April, May and June.
Make a little song,
With a little tune.
Sing a little song,
With a little tune.
Put July and August and September,
With October, November and December.
That's the year for you,
That's the year for you.

## 5 Meet some children

Read

Listen

John lives in the town. He lives in a flat.
It has got two bedrooms, a living room,
a kitchen and a bathroom.

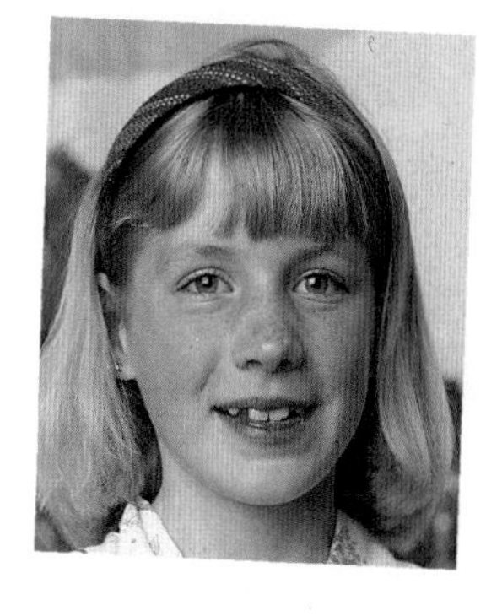
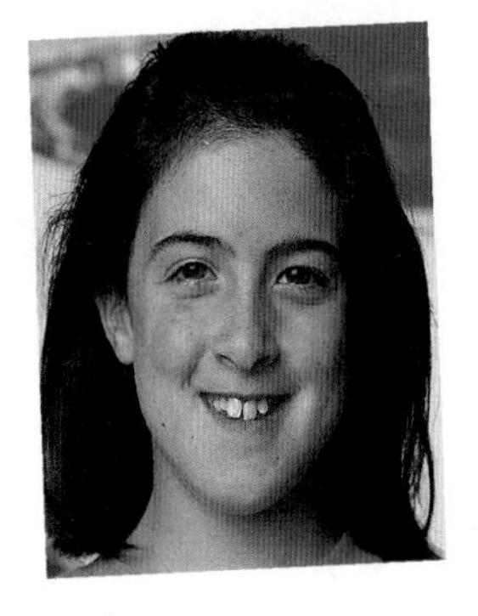

**1** John  **2** Sara  **3** Anna  **4** James

Where do they live?
What are these childrens' homes like?

A.B. p.23

Listen and answer the questions in your Action Book.

## 6 Diaries

A.B. p.25

Fill in your diary in your Action Book.
Write *one* thing on each day. Hide it from your partner.

Listen

Ask
and answer

What did you do on Monday?
Did you watch TV?

Fill in your partner's diary in your Action Book.

# Factfile
## Inventions

William Heath Robinson, the artist, drew this picture. How does this machine work?

The two men at the top look for litter. When they see litter, they pull the string. The string rings the bell. The driver goes to the litter. The glue falls on the wheel. The litter sticks to the wheel. The man picks up the litter with a fork. Then he puts it in the bin.

Is this a useful invention?

*Useful inventions*

The Earl of Sandwich, an Englishman, loved card games. He did not want to stop the game at dinnertime. He asked for some meat in two pieces of bread. It was the first sandwich!

An American, Whitcomb L. Judson, did not like buttons. He invented a chain of teeth. It was the first zip!

Which jobs in the house don't you like?
Invent a useful machine for these jobs.
Draw the machine in your ET book. Write how it works.

*Four famous inventors*

Alexander Graham Bell, an American, invented the telephone.

John Logie Baird, a Scottish man, invented the TV.

Charles Babbage, an English scientist, invented this machine.
Can you guess what it is?

The Italian inventor, Guglielmo Marconi, sent the first radio message from England to America.

It's the first computer!

Find out about a famous inventor in your country.
What did he or she invent?

# Unit 7

## 1 California

Listen and look

Read

Act

It was very cold in Cliff Castle.

Computer: What game do you want to play today?

Emma: 'California'. It's hot there.

Beth: C-a-l, How do you spell 'California'? Has it got one 'l' or two?

Emma: One. It's C-a-l-i-f-o-r-n-i-a.

Joe: This isn't California. This is the new planet again. Look at those giant trees!

Al: Don't be silly! We're in Yosemite National Park. These are redwood trees.
Beth: How tall are they?
Al: A hundred metres! And they're two thousand years old!
Joe: Look! 'Don't feed the bears.'
Emma: Ooh! Bears!

Tammy: Yes – black bears!
Al: That's right – 'There are black bears in . . .'
Beth: Quick! Run over the bridge!
Joe: No – through the trees!
Emma: Don't move! I've got the black box!

## 2 How tall is the bear?

Look

Listen

Practise

**A:** How tall is the bear?
**B:** It's 250 centimetres tall. How tall is Al?

Now ask about Beth, Joe, Emma, Tammy and Cleo.

How tall are you?
How tall is your partner?

Write the answers in your ET book.

## 3 Print your name on a T-shirt!

Listen
Say

ABCDEFGHIJKLM
NOPQRSTUVWXYZ

Listen
Practise

Emma: I want my name on my T-shirt please!
Man: What's your name?
Emma: Emma.
Man: How do you spell that?
Emma: E-m-m-a.

With your partner, ask for your name on a T-shirt.
Now ask for your sister's, brother's, friend's, teacher's name.

## 4 Don't do that, Tammy!

Listen
Practise

Partner **A**, you are Tammy. Partner **B**, you are Al.

climb that tree

eat that mushroom

jump in the lake

press the button

feed the bears

Tammy: I want to climb that tree.
Al: Don't climb that tree, Tammy!

## 5 We're going on a bear hunt!

Listen

Say
and do

We're going on a bear hunt.
I'm not afraid. Not me!

Grass! Long, green grass!
We can't go over it.
We can't go under it.
So we're going through it.
Swish! Swish! Swish! Swish!

A wood! Big, tall trees!
We can't go over the trees . . .
Crash! Crash! Crash! Crash!

A cave! A big, dark cave!
We can't go over it . . .
Boom! Boom! Boom! Boom!

Two black eyes. Long, white teeth
A bear! Quick!
Through the cave, (Boom! . . .)
Through the trees, (Crash! . . .)
Through the grass, (Swish! . . .)
Back home and
shut the door. (Bang!)

## 6 Feed the bees!

Listen

Say

Feed the bees with
three sweet peas.

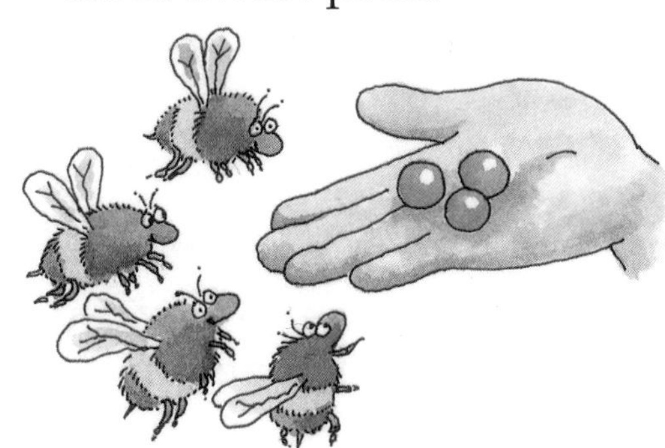

Give the pigs
six big chips.

# Unit 8

## 1 Hollywood

Listen and look

Read

Act

Today Joe and Emma want to play the 'Hollywood' game.

Joe: They're making a film! How exciting! I'm going to watch.
Emma: You can't go in there, Joe. They're filming.
Man: Lights! Camera! Action!

Emma: Oh stop! You're going to kill the girl! She's hurt!

Emma: Oh no! The dragon's going to eat Joe! Look out!

Emma: Are you going to be OK, Joe? Is she OK?
Joe: Don't be silly, Em. We're fine.

Man: You were very good. You're going to be a filmstar, young man!

## 2 What's going to happen?

Look and say

The girl
The rocks
The dragon
The spiders

fall
hit
eat

**A:** The girl is going to fall . . .

## 3 Let's go to the cinema!

Listen and look

Read

Joe: Let's go and see this! I love horror films!
Emma: Oh no! Horror films are awful! I like musicals.
Beth: I don't like musicals. They're boring.
Adventure films are great!
Al: Look, there's a comedy. I like comedies.
Tammy: I want to see 'Toots the Duck'. I like cartoons!

## 4 Which films do they want to see?

Listen

Ask and answer

**A:** Which film does Joe want to see?
**B:** The horror film. Which film does Emma want to see?

Ask about Beth, Al and Tammy.

## 5 When does the film start?

Listen

Ask and answer

**A:** When does the horror film start?
**B:** At two o'clock. When does it finish?
**A:** At four o'clock.

A.B. p.32

Look at page 32 in your Action Book. Which films do you and your partner like?

## 6 Make a fortune-teller

Write
Listen
Play

Make a fortune-teller.
Write fortunes.

You are going to be a filmstar.
You are going to live 100 years.
You are going to be a teacher.
You are going to be a doctor.
You are going to be an engineer.
You are going to be a pop singer.
You are going to fall off your bike.
You are going to be a footballer.

## 7 Meet some children

Guess

What are they going to be?

Maria

Paul

Adam

Lisa

Listen

A.B. p.33

Listen and answer the questions in your Action Book.

# Factfile
## Film tricks

Monsters in films are not real monsters. They are usually small models. Sometimes they are machines. Sometimes there are people in the machines.

Bottles are not real glass. They are made of sugar. You can break these bottles easily and they do not hurt you.

Joe's dragon had a plastic head, shoulders and arms. A man pressed buttons and moved the mouth, the eyes and the arms.

Windows are made of sugar, too.

Blood is not real blood. It is red paint. This actor had red paint in a small bag under his clothes. He pressed the bag and the paint came out.

Spiders' webs are not real spiders' webs. They are made of glue.

In this film the boy seems very small. How do they do it?

The boy isn't really small, the scissors are very big!

Here is a poster for a horror film. Draw a picture story about two children and the monster snowmen.
Write what is happening in your pictures.

# Unit 9

## 1 Alaska

Listen and look

Read

Act

California was hot and sunny.
Now the children choose 'Alaska'.
It's cold and snowy there.

Emma: It's beautiful! It's white and clean and new.
Joe: But it's very cold.
Beth: Sh! Look at that baby seal!
Can you see it?
Emma: No . . . Oh yes, it's white like the snow.
Tammy: Look at those big seals.
I want to see them!

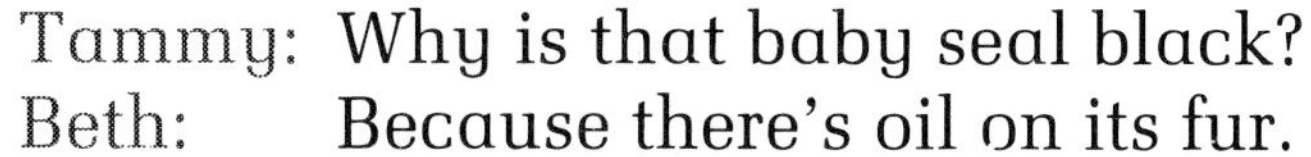

Tammy: Why is that baby seal black?
Beth: Because there's oil on its fur.
Emma: Poor thing! What can we do?

Al: Let's take it to the Rescue Centre. Come on!
Emma: Look at the poor mother. She wants her baby.
Joe: We can take her, too!

## 2 Let's help!

Listen

Practise

With your partner, take it in turns to be Beth and Joe.
Choose Joe's words from the box.

| Let's help it! | Let's help him! |
| --- | --- |
| Let's help her! | Let's help them! |

Beth: The seal is dying.
Joe: Let's help it!

Beth: The men are cleaning the seal.

Beth: The girl is feeding the seal.

Beth: Al is putting the seals in the sea.

## 3 Why?

Listen

Read

| | |
|---|---|
| Tammy: | Why is the baby seal black? |
| Beth: | Because there's oil on its fur, Tammy. |
| Tammy: | Why is there oil on its fur? |
| Beth: | Because there's oil in the sea, Tammy. |
| Tammy: | Why is there oil in the sea? |
| Beth: | Because there was a hole in an oil tanker, Tammy. |
| Tammy: | Why was there a hole? |
| Beth: | Because it hit a rock under the sea, Tammy. |
| Tammy: | Why did it hit a rock? |
| Beth: | Oh Tammy, be quiet! |
| Tammy: | Why? |

Practise — Take it in turns to be Tammy and Beth.

## 4 Why did the children laugh?

Listen

Read

Ask and answer

1 Tammy was hungry. She took Joe's sandwich.

2 Joe was angry. He took Tammy's hat.

3 Tammy was cold. She took Beth's scarf.

4 Beth chased Tammy.

5 Tammy fell in the snow. The children laughed.

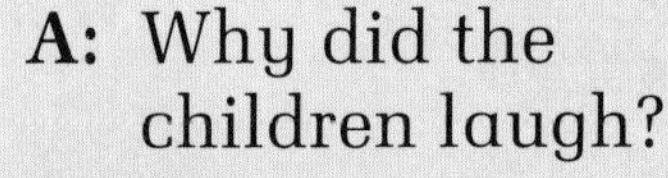

**A:** Why did the children laugh?
**B:** Because Tammy fell in the snow.
**B:** Why did Tammy fall in the snow?
**A:** Because . . .

## 5 Clean the beach

Look
Play

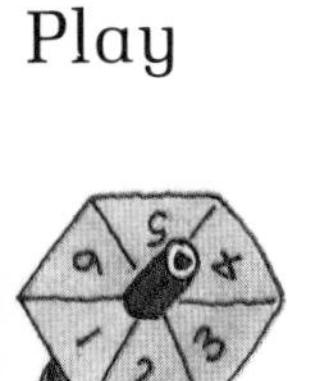


1 a plastic bag
2 a bottle
3 a can
4 a newspaper
5 oil
6 nothing

A.B. p.37

Look at the beach. It is dirty. There is oil on the beach. There are plastic bags, bottles, cans and a newspaper.

Can you and your partner clean the beach in five minutes? Spin your spinner and pick up the litter. Cross out the things in your Action Book.

## 6 The future's in our hands

Listen
Sing

We want to see blue seas,
We want to see green trees,
We are defenders of our lands.
We want to breathe clean air,
We want to show we care,
We know the future's in our hands.

We want to see birds fly,
Up into a clear sky,
We are defenders of our lands,
We want to see flowers grow,
To pollution we say 'NO!'
We know the future's in our hands.

# Unit 10

## 1 The Cliff Castle Diamonds

Listen and look

Read

Act

Colin: This is Lady Jane Forbes, my great-great-great grandmother.
She's wearing the Cliff Castle Diamonds.

Joe: Where are the diamonds now?

Colin: We don't know.

Joe: I'm going to find the diamonds!
Beth: Where are you going to look?
Al: Look at these letters on the picture. What do they say?
Emma: I think it's a secret code.

Emma: I can read it! Uncle Colin, where's the dungeon?
Colin: The dungeon? Why?
Emma: Because I think the diamonds are in the dungeon.
Colin: I'm sorry, Emma. There isn't a dungeon in Cliff Castle.

## 2 The secret code

Look

Read

Why does Emma think the diamonds are in the dungeon?
Can *you* read the message?
Here's a clue:

**EJBNPOE** = Diamond

This message is in the code. Can you read it with your partner?

UIFSF JT OP EVOHFPO JO DMJGG DBTUMF OPX
CVU UIFSF XBT B EVOHFPO JO UIF PME EBZT.

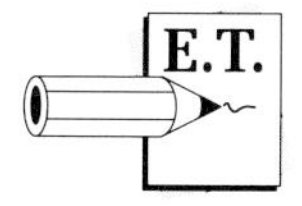

Now write a message in the code.
Can your partner read it?

# 3 The old castle

Read

Cliff Castle is very old.
This was the downstairs in the old days:

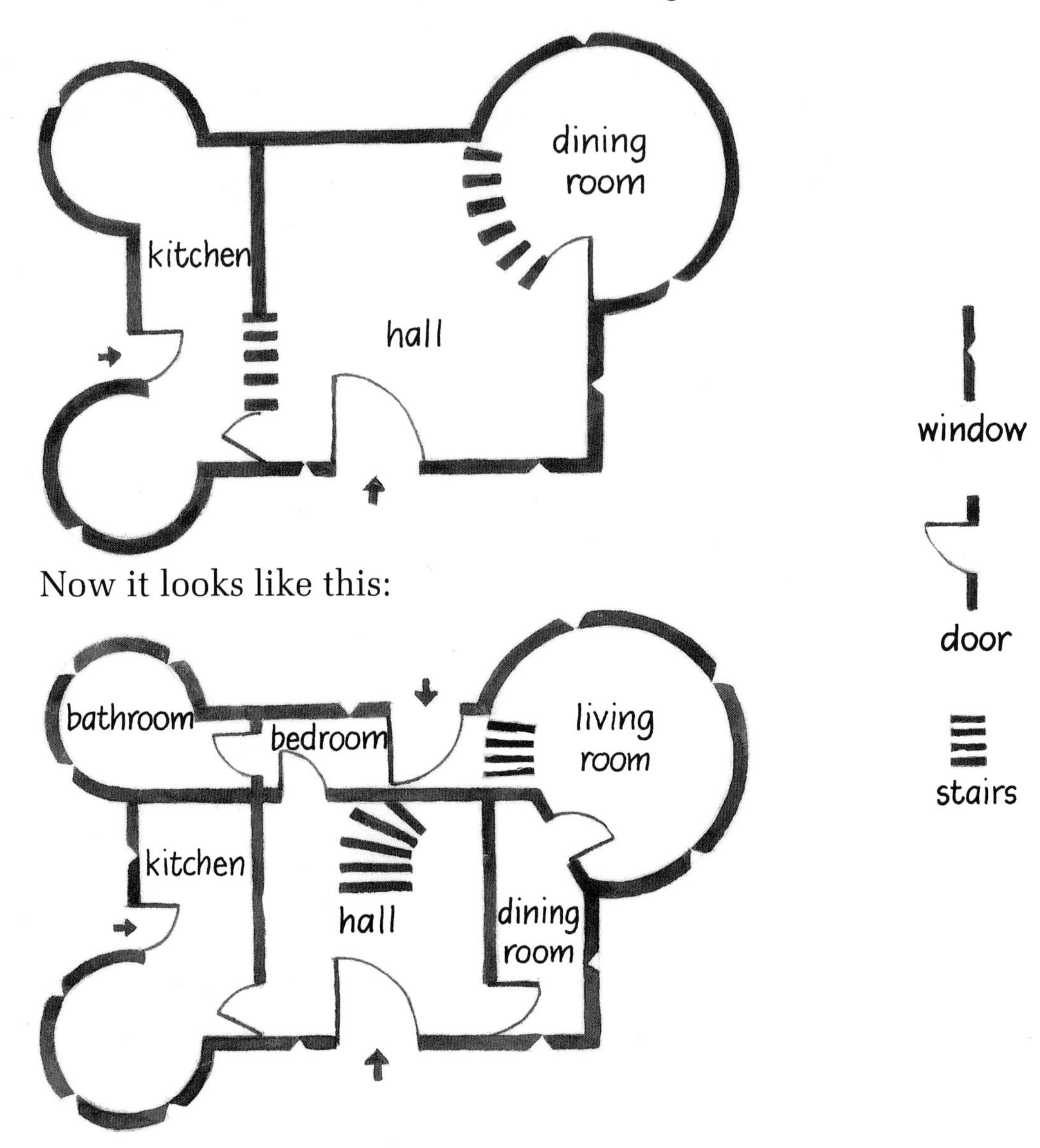


Now it looks like this:

Look and say

How many differences can you find?
Write them in your ET book.

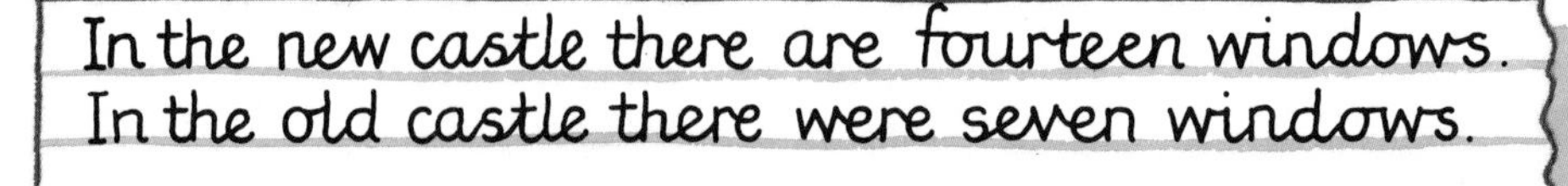


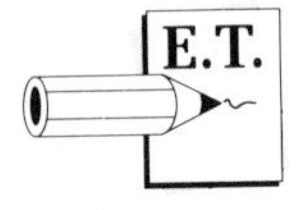


Where was the dungeon?

## 4 The dungeon

Listen

Read

Look

Write

The children looked at the old picture.
Al said, 'Look at these stairs. I think they went down to the dungeon. Where are they now? Are they in the kitchen or in the hall?'

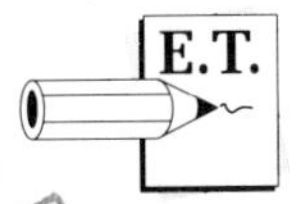


Look at the pictures, then write what happened.

Joe: It's a huge diamond!
Al: No, it's only a glass ball.

These words can help you:

look open find go

*The children looked under the carpet in the hall.*
*Then they looked...*

# Factfile

## The Arctic

The Arctic is the land and sea at the top of the world. Look in the sky at night and you can see these stars, the Bear.

The Greek word *arktos* means 'bear' and the Arctic is under the Bear.

In winter the Arctic is very cold and dark, because the sun does not rise there. In summer the sun does not go down at night. In this photo the sun is shining at midnight.

It is very, very cold in the Arctic winter. When you cry, the tears freeze on your face. When you throw water in the air, it freezes.

The Inuit people live in the Arctic. They use sledges and dogs. In the Inuit language, there are twenty-six words for 'snow'. How many words are there in your language for 'snow'?

Arctic animals have a difficult life. In winter there is ice and snow everywhere. Some animals, like polar bears, have very thick fur. This keeps them warm.

There is very little food. Some animals – the reindeer and the birds – move to warmer places.

Some animals change colour in the winter. The fox and the hare turn white. Other animals cannot see them in the snow.

Make a paper snowflake.

**1** Draw a big circle.

**2** Fold the paper three times.

**3** Cut out shapes.

**4** Open the paper.

# Unit 11

## 1 Back to the past

Listen and look

Read

Act

Emma: I want to go to Wales.
Beth: You pressed the yellow button!
We always press the red button.

Wales

Can we wash? Our hands are dirty.

At night they finished late.
They were very tired. Their clothes, faces, hands and feet were very dirty.

An old woman gave them a bowl of grey soup and a piece of black bread.

Joe: Can I have another bowl of soup, please? I'm very hungry.
Old woman: No. Sit down.

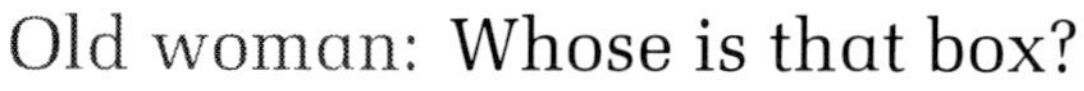

Old woman: Whose is that box? Give it to me.
Al: No! It's Emma's.
Beth: Quick! Press the green button!

Emma: That was awful!
Joe: I'm glad we didn't live in the past.

## 2 Our/their

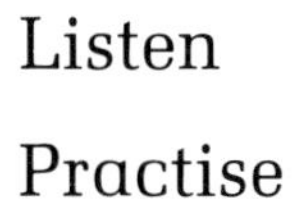

Listen

Practise

**1** hands

**2** faces

**3** clothes

**4** feet

Old woman: What's the matter?
Emma and Beth: Our hands are dirty.
Old woman: What?
Joe: Their hands are dirty.

## 3 Whose is it?

Look

Listen

Ask
and answer

**A:** Whose doll's house is it?
**B:** The big girl's.

## 4 Can I have another bowl of soup, please?

Listen

Practise

bowl of soup

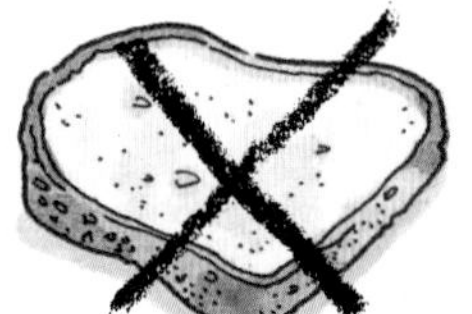

piece of bread

glass of milk

cup of tea

glass of water

bottle of lemonade

**A:** Can I have another bowl of soup, please?
**B:** Yes, of course. Here you are./Sorry. There's no more.

## 5 The children in the mine

Listen

Read

There were twenty-four children in the coal mine. They got up at three o'clock every day. They had a small piece of bread and a cup of water for breakfast, then they went to the mine. They worked hard all day. They finished late at night. They were always tired and always hungry. The children slept in one room. There were two small windows in it and it was very cold. They slept on the floor in their clothes. The old woman locked the door at night. She sometimes hit the children with a big stick and they were all afraid of her.

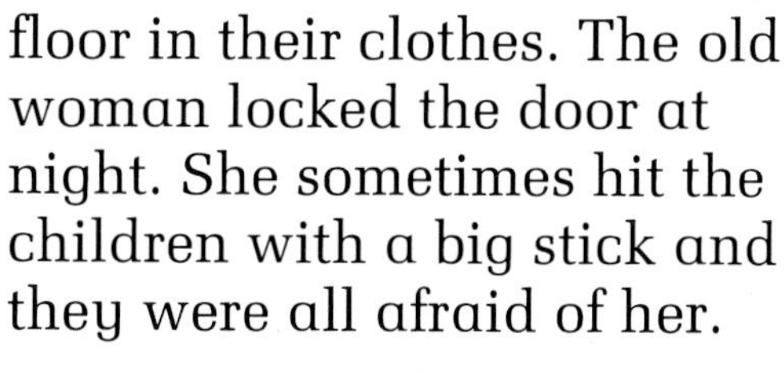

Ask and answer

**1** How many children were there in the mine?
**2** What time did they get up?
**3** What did they have for breakfast?
**4** When did they finish work?
**5** Were they happy?
**6** Where did they sleep?
**7** What was the room like?
**8** What did the old woman do at night?
**9** Why were they all afraid of her?

## 6 Batty Betty

Listen

Say

Batty Betty, my pet cat,
Goes to bed in a big,
black hat.

# Unit 12

## 1 The World Cup

Listen and look

Read

Act

Al is playing with the computer. He chooses 'Football' and presses the blue button.

Al is in the future! He is a footballer and he is playing in the World Cup. The match is Brazil – England and Al is in the English team.

The match started at three o'clock. At half past three the Brazilian team scored a goal.

At quarter to four it was half time. The score was one – nil to Brazil.

It's now ten to five. A man is talking on the television. Listen!

Can the English team score a goal? The Brazilians have got the ball. Peres is passing it to Mendes . . . But Al, the English player, is next to Mendes . . .

Al is running in front of Mendes . . . and he's got the ball!

Al is running fast. Number 8, the Brazilian, is behind Al – can he stop him? No! Al is too fast . . .

Al is in front of the goal. The Brazilian goalkeeper is waiting . . . Al is going to shoot . . . He shoots . . . And it's a goal! It's a goal!

And that's the whistle! So it's one all. That was a wonderful game and a wonderful goal!

## 2 When did the match start?

Look

Read

**1** The match started.

**2** Brazil scored.

**3** Half time started.

**4** The match started again.

**5** England scored.

**6** The match finished

Listen

Ask and answer

**A:** When did the match start?
**B:** At three o'clock.

## 3 Which goalkeeper is English?

Listen

Say

English
Spanish
Brazilian
American
Italian

Ask and answer

**A:** Which goalkeeper is English?
**B:** Number 1.

## 4 The English team

Look

Read

The referee is in front of number 6.
Number 8 is behind number 6.
Number 2 is next to number 6.

Listen

Practise

**A:** Who's in front of number 8?
**B:** Number 6.

Listen

Say

## 5 Football rhymes

One, two, three, four.
Which team are we shouting for?
S-c-o-t-l-a-n-d – Scotland!

Five, six, seven, eight.
Which team do we think is great?
A-r-g-e-n-t-i-n-a – Argentina!

# Factfile

## The Olympic Games

*The first Olympic Games*

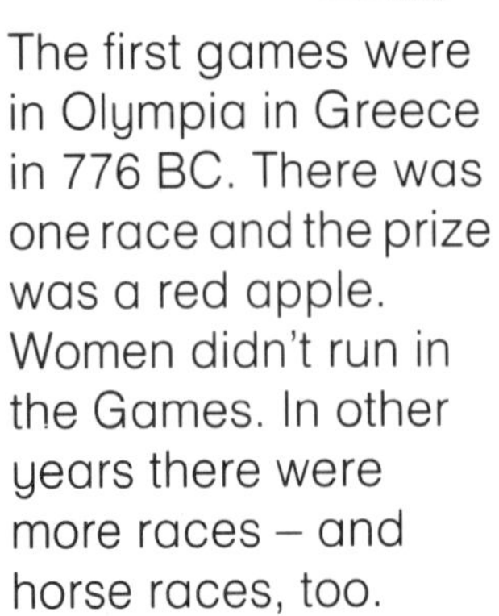

The first games were in Olympia in Greece in 776 BC. There was one race and the prize was a red apple. Women didn't run in the Games. In other years there were more races – and horse races, too.

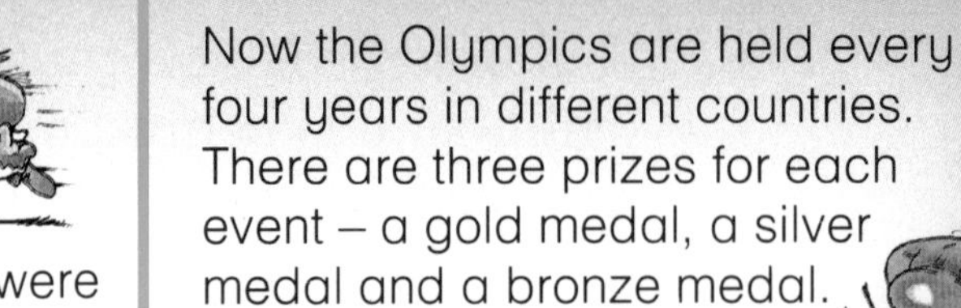

Now the Olympics are held every four years in different countries. There are three prizes for each event – a gold medal, a silver medal and a bronze medal.

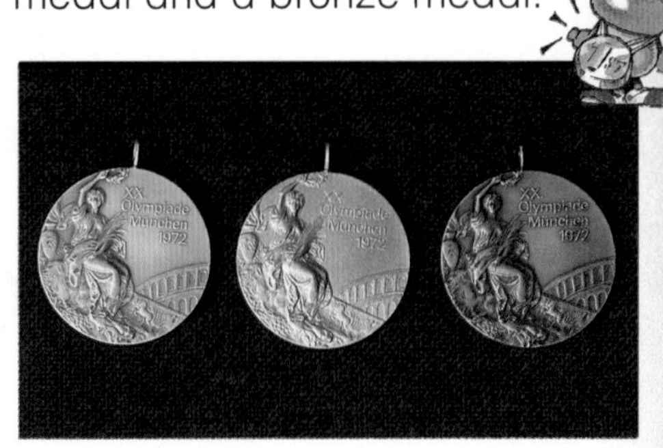

Every new Olympic Games has new sports. Today you can watch athletics, boxing, canoeing, cycling, basketball, football, gymnastics, swimming and many other sports.

Ski jumping, skiing and skating are events in the Winter Olympic Games.

Which sports can you play?
What is your favourite sport?
Ask your friends. Write.

*Some Olympic facts*

Johnny Weissmuller, the swimmer, won three gold medals in Paris in 1924 and two in Amsterdam in 1928. He then went to Hollywood and became the first Tarzan in films.

Nadia Comaneci from Romania had the first perfect score – ten points. She scored it in gymnastics when she was fifteen.

These days there is always an Olympic mascot. This is 'Cobi', the mascot for Barcelona in 1992.

The Olympic flag has five coloured rings.
The colours are blue, yellow, black, green and red on white, because every country in the world has one of these colours on its flag. So, the Olympic flag means the countries are friends.

1. The Olympic Games are going to be held in your country. Draw a new flag. What is your mascot?
2. Find out about the last Olympic Games. Where and when were they? How many medals did your country win? In which sports? Write about it.
3. Write about a famous athlete in your country.

# Unit 13

## 1 African safari

Listen and look

Read

Act

Beth wanted to play 'African safari'.

The children were on safari in Africa.
Jomo was their driver.
They saw lots of animals.
They saw some lions, some zebras and some monkeys, but they didn't see any elephants. Beth loved elephants.

They went a long way. Then they saw a baby elephant. He was alone.
'Where is his mother?' asked Joe.
'Some men killed her,' said Jomo. 'They sell the tusks and people give them lots of money.'

They heard a noise. Then they saw the men.
'There they are!' shouted Joe. 'Let's catch them!'
'Be careful!' said Jomo. 'These men are dangerous!'
'Oh no! They've got guns!' said Emma.
'Where's the black box? Press the button, Beth!' said Al.
'What about Jomo?' asked Beth.
'Hold his hand. Let's take him too!' said Joe.

## 2 Beth loves elephants

Look

Here is Beth in her bedroom.

Listen

Ask and answer

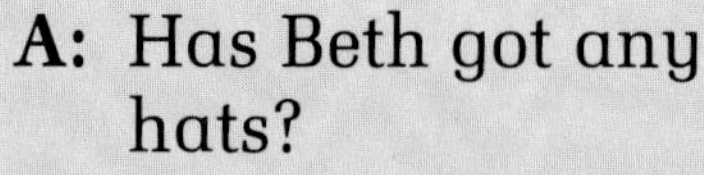

**A:** Has Beth got any hats?
**B:** Yes. Has she got any cups?

Ask about hats, cups, pictures, games, socks, videos, rubbers, books and T-shirts.

E.T.

Then write in your ET books like this:

*Beth has got some...*
*She hasn't got any...*

## 3 The safari game

Read

Play

**1** Write two names . . .

. . . Fold your paper.

. . . Give it to your partner.

**2** Write a country . . .

an elephant

**3** Write an animal . . .

**4** Write what the people said . . .

**5** Write what the animal did . . .

Batman and Robin
went to Alaska
They saw an elephant
They said Hello!
It climbed a tree
Then they went home.

**6** Open your papers and read.

## 4 Elephants

**Ask and answer**

**Guess**

Take it in turns to ask your partner these questions:

How tall are elephants?
What do they eat?
Where do they live?
What colour are they?
Why do people kill them?
What do people do with their tusks?
When do the babies leave their mothers?

**A Joke**

What's the difference between an Indian elephant and an African elephant?

A: About 5000 kilometres.

Now turn your books upside down and read about elephants. Were you right?

Elephants live in Africa and India. They eat grass and leaves. The babies leave their mothers when they are fifteen years old. They live for sixty or seventy years. They are grey. They are three to four metres tall. People kill elephants because they want their tusks. They sell the tusks. People make presents and ornaments from the tusks.

# Unit 14

## 1 Going home

Listen and look

Read

Act

Jomo: Where am I? It's very cold here.
Emma: It's OK. You're in Scotland. You're safe here.
Jomo: What's happening?
Al: It's snowing!

Joe: We're going home tomorrow, Jomo. What are you going to do?
Al: Do you want to live here?
Jomo: No, thank you! It's too cold. I don't know anybody here. I want to go back to Africa.
Beth: You can go to Africa by plane.
Jomo: But I haven't got any money here.

Joe: Everything is wrong – Jomo wants to go home, but he can't go. We're going home tomorrow, but we don't want to go. We didn't see the Castle ghost and we didn't find the Cliff Castle Diamonds.
Emma: Oh dear!

## 2 Do you know anybody in Scotland?

Read

Al knows somebody in Scotland. His uncle lives there.
Jomo doesn't know anybody in Scotland.

Listen

America

England

Australia

France

Germany

Ask and answer

**A:** Do you know anybody in Scotland?
**B:** No. Do you know anybody in America?
**A:** Yes, I know somebody in America. My cousin lives there.

## 3 What is Jomo going to do?

Read

Look and write

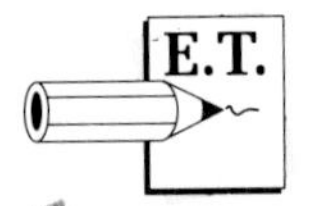


Jomo doesn't want to live in Scotland.
He can't go back to Africa by plane.
What is he going to do?
Look at the pictures then write Jomo's story in your ET books.

Jomo/go/secret room.

type/African Safari

press/button

go back/Africa

men/chase Jomo

go/town

see/police

catch/men

feed/baby elephant.

Jomo is going to go into the secret room...

## 4 A huge, hungry hippo

Listen

Sing

A huge, hungry hippo
is walking down the road,
Left, right, left, right,
He's walking down
the road.

Two tired tigers and
a huge, hungry hippo
Are walking down the road,
Left, right, left, right,
They're walking down
the road.

Three thirsty panthers . . .
Four fast frogs . . .
Five fat flies . . .
Six slippery snakes . . .
Seven small spiders . . .
Eight elegant elephants . . .
Nine nice mice . . .
Ten tiny tortoises . . .

## 5 Do butterflies like rainy weather?

Listen

rainy snowy sunny

Ask
and answer

**A:** Do butterflies like rainy weather?
**B:** No, they like sunny weather.
Do snakes like snowy weather?

# Factfile
## Animals in danger

These animals are extinct. They lived in the old days, but there are no mammoths, no dodos and no quaggas today. Hunters killed them all. Many animals today are in danger. We must help them or they are going to be extinct, too.

Some animals are in danger because people hunt them. People kill wild cats, snakes and crocodiles because they want their skins.

Some animals are in danger because people catch them and sell them for pets.

*How are people helping these animals?*

Laws now say you can't buy or sell elephant tusks or rare animals or their skins. Police catch these shop-keepers and put them in prison.

*What can we do?*

Don't buy presents or toys made from rare animals. Don't keep these animals as pets.

Some animals are in danger because people are cutting down trees and destroying their homes. Some countries now have National Parks. Scientists sometimes move animals to these parks. The animals are safe, because people can't cut down the trees or kill the animals.

In New Zealand scientists saved the black robin. There were only four male black robins and one female in the world. The female's name was 'Old Blue'. When she laid eggs, the scientists gave the eggs to other birds. These birds looked after the baby robins. 'Old Blue' saw her empty nest and she laid more eggs. Now there are more than sixty black robins.

A lot of groups work to save the animals. You can join the World Wide Fund for Nature or Friends of the Earth. You can help too!

Friends of the Earth

Choose an animal in danger and find out everything about it.
Where does it live?
What does it eat?
How many are there in the world today?
Why is it in danger?
What can you do to help it?

# Unit 15

## 1 The ghost

Listen and look

Read

Act

It's the children's last night in Cliff Castle.
It is late.
Joe and Al are tired. They are going to bed.

Al: Joe, look at the clock!
It was quarter past twelve and now it's twelve o'clock.
The clock's going backwards!

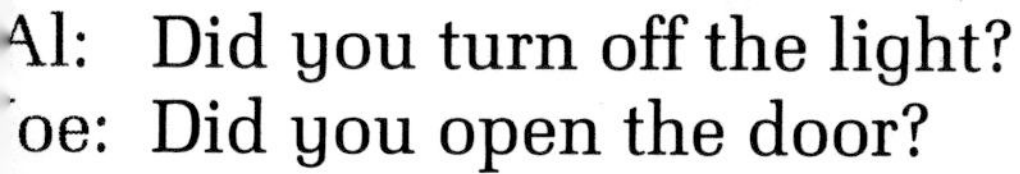
Al: Did you turn off the light?
Joe: Did you open the door?

Al: There's somebody in the room!
Quick, give me the torch!

Joe: Did you see him?
Al: It wasn't a man – it was a woman. She was next to the door.
Joe: What was she like?
Al: She had long, blonde hair.
I know her face.
Where did I see that face?
I know! It's Uncle Colin's great-great-great grandmother.
It's Lady Jane!
Joe: Aagh! It's the ghost!

## 2 What did the ghost do?

Look

This was Al and Joe's room at eleven o'clock.
Look at the picture on page 74.
That is their room at twelve o'clock.
Find ten differences.

Say

She moved the picture. It was next to the door, now it's next to the window.

What did the ghost take?

## 3 A rhyme

Listen and say

Yesterday on the stair
I saw a man who wasn't there.
He wasn't there again today.
I hope he's going to go away!

## 4 The glass ball

Listen and look

Read

Lady Jane went into the hall.
Al and Joe followed her.

She went to her picture.
She put the glass ball in the hole under the picture.

Then she disappeared through the wall.

Al looked at the ball but Joe looked *through* it.

He saw a secret cupboard behind the picture.
The Cliff Castle Diamonds were in the cupboard!

Say

Now close your books and tell the story like this:

**A:** Lady Jane went into the hall.
**B:** Joe and Al followed her.

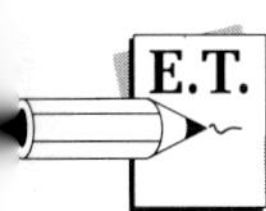


Write the story in your ET book.

# *Key words and expressions*

**Unit 1**
winter
Scotland
train
mountain
fun
windsurf
tree
in the holidays
by the sea
at home
in the mountains
in the country

**Unit 2**
castle
uncle
grandpa
cousin
aunt
England
Ireland
Wales
live
send
wall
door
window
clock
Come in.
Wait and see!

**Scotland factfile**
beautiful
high
deep
ski
kilt
bagpipes
dinosaur
neck
seal
scientist
extinct

**Unit 3**
*Rooms in a house*
living room
kitchen
dining room
bedroom
bathroom
toilet
hall
garden

stairs
upstairs
downstairs
want
bookshelf
button
press
go in
secret
giant
computer
key (computer)
happen
flat
What is it like?
in the town

**Unit 4**
type
space
new
planet
spaceship
seatbelt
pick up
key (door)
ring (n)
magic
chose
stood
about
Just a minute.

**Space factfile**
astronaut
water
keep fit
first
grow
thin
fat
web
pack
tray
magnet
oven
washbasin
hole
inside
soap

**Unit 5**
world
Earth
Africa
India
Australia
suddenly
saw
land (v)
had
rainbow
round (prep)
beautiful
flower
mushroom
teddy bear
doll
awful
noise
mouse/mice

**Unit 6**
more
found
machine
back (n)
took
made
camera
parrot
diary
Look and see!

*Months*
January
February
March
April
May
June
July
August
September
October
November
December

**Inventions factfile**
artist
litter
string
ring (v)
bell
driver
glue
wheel
stick
useful
sandwich
invent
chain
zip
famous
telephone
send
message

**Unit 7**
spell (v)
National Park
redwood
hundred
thousand
(11) years old
bear
over
through
bridge
eye test
pot
seed
plastic bag
Quick!

**Unit 8**
lights
kill
hit
hurt (adj)
fine
cinema
horror film
musical
adventure
comedy
cartoon
fortune-teller
turn over

*Jobs*
filmstar
doctor
engineer
pop singer
footballer

Look out!

**Film tricks factfile**
real
models
glass
made of
sugar
break
blood

**Unit 9**
snow(y)
oil
fur
Rescue Centre
tanker
scarf
chase
laugh
can (n)
newspaper
litter
polar bear
future
pollution
Poor thing!

**Unit 10**
diamond
great grandmother
code
dungeon
message
clue
hink
carpet
ous
oy
alk
omorrow

**Arctic factfile**
and
shine
nidnight
cry
ears
reeze
sledge
hick
varm
eindeer
ox

hare
snowflake

**Unit 11**
past (n)
early
coal mine
all day
hard (adv)
push
at night
late
tired
gave
soup
a piece of
another
glad
lemonade
lock
stick (n)
moustache
beard
What's the matter?
Give it to me.

**Unit 12**
match
World Cup
Brazil
team
score
goal
talk
pass
fast
goalkeeper
wait
shoot
whistle
wonderful

*Nationalities*
Brazilian
Spanish
American
Italian
German
Greek
Turkish
French

from
speak
referee

get home
programme
channel
one-nil
one all
half time

**Olympics factfile**
held
each
event
medal
gold
silver
bronze

*Sports*
athletics
boxing
cycling
basketball
gymnastics
swimming
skiing
skating
ski-jumping

other
won
became
point (n)
flag
mascot
last
athlete

**Unit 13**
safari
lion
zebra
elephant
sell
tusk
money
hear(d)
catch
dangerous
gun
hold/held
leaves (n)
leave (v)
ornament
a long way
Be careful!

**Unit 14**
safe
go back
everything
police
left
right
Oh dear!

**Animals in danger factfile**
mammoth
dodo
hunter
hunt
crocodile
skin
law
rare
shopkeeper
prison
cut down
destroy
save
male
female

**Unit 15**
last
backwards
turn off
follow
disappear

**Longman Group UK Limited,**
*Longman House, Burnt Mill, Harlow,*
*Essex CM20 2JE, England*
*and Associated Companies throughout the world.*



First published 1992
ISBN 0 582 02037 9

Set in Linotronic 300 Melior 14/16 pt.

Printed in Great Britain
by Cambus Litho

**Acknowledgements**

We are grateful to the following for permission to reproduce photographic and illustrative material in this book:

Ace Photo Agency for pages 10 (top left), 30 (top left) and 72 (bottom); Bryan and Cherry Alexander for page 52 (bottom right); Allsport for page 62 (top left and bottom left); Alpha Photographic Press Agency Limited for page 42 (top right); Arctic Camera for page 52 (bottom left); Bruce Coleman Limited for pages 6 (top middle, top right, bottom left and bottom right), 53 (bottom) and 72 (top); Colorsport for pages 62 (bottom right) and 63 (top right); Gerald Duckworth and Company Limited for page 32 (left); Mary Evans Picture Library for page 56 (bottom left); Format Partners – Photo Library/Jacky Chapman for page 41 (right); Friends of the Earth Photo Library for page 73 (bottom); The Ronald Grant Archive for pages 43 and 63 (top left); Susan Griggs Agency/Ian Yeomans for page 30 (bottom middle); Robert Harding Picture Library for page 52 (top right); The Hulton Picture Company for pages 13, 22 (top left), 33 (top left) and 56 (top left and top middle left); Frank Lane Picture Agency Limited for pages 46 and 73 (middle); Museum of Childhood, Edinburgh for page 56 (bottom middle right); Network Photographers/Barry Lewis for page 31 (left); Novosti for page 22 (bottom left)); Oxford Scientific Films Limited for page 67; St John Pope for pages 31 (middle left, middle right and right) and 41 (left, middle left and middle right); Popperfoto for page 62 (top right); Rex Features Limited for pages 22 (top right), 42 (top left and bottom right), 53 (top right) and 62 (middle left); the Trustees of the Science Museum for page 33 (bottom right); Science Photo Library for pages 22 (bottom right), 32 (right) and 33 (top middle, top right and bottom left); Sefton Photo Library for page 10 (bottom right); Sporting Pictures UK Limited for page 63 (bottom right); Tony Stone Photo Library – London for pages 12 (bottom left), 53 (top left), 62 (middle right) and 63 (bottom left); the Board of Trustees of the V&A for page 56 (top middle right, top right, bottom middle left and bottom right); Zefa for pages 10 (top right and bottom left), 12 (top right and bottom right) and 73 (top).
Picture research by Vanessa Kelly.

**Illustrated by** Jan Lewis
with Alexander, Kathy Baxendale, Mik Brown, Heather Clarke, Caroline Ewen, Rosemary Murphy and Jo Wright.